ISBN: 0-8378-2011-1

The Hymn of St. Francis

St. Francis of Assisi

The C. R. Gibson Company
Norwalk, Connecticut

The Canticle Of The Sun

O most high, almighty, good Lord god, to thee belong praise, glory, honor, and all blessing!

Praise ye the Lord. Praise ye the Lord from the heavens: praise him in the heights.

Praise ye him, all his angels: praise ye him, all his hosts.

Praise ye him, sun and moon: praise him, all ye stars of light.

Praise him, ye heavens of heavens, and ye waters that be above the heavens.

Let them praise the name of the Lord: for he commanded, and they were created.

He hath also stablished them for ever and ever: he hath made a decree which shall not pass.

Praise the Lord from the earth, ye dragons, and all deeps:

Fire, and hail; snow, and vapour; stormy wind fulfilling his word:

Mountains, and all hills; fruitful trees, and all cedars:

Beasts, and all cattle; creeping things, and flying fowl:

Kings of the earth, and all people; princes, and all judges of the earth:

Both young men, and maidens; old men, and children:

Let them praise the name of the Lord: for his name alone is excellent; his glory is above the earth and heaven.

PSALM 148:1-13

Praised be my Lord God with all his
creatures; and specially our brother the
sun, who brings us the day, and who
brings us the light; fair is he, and shining
with a very great splendor: O Lord,
to us he signifies thee!

And God made two great lights; the greater light to
rule the day, and the lesser light to rule the night:
he made the stars also.
And God set them in the firmament of the heaven to
give light upon the earth,
And to rule over the day and over the night, and to
divide the light from the darkness: and God saw
that it was good.

GENESIS 1:16-18

The day is thine, the night also is thine: thou
hast prepared the light and the sun.
Thou hast set all the borders of the earth: thou
hast made summer and winter.

PSALM 74:16,17

I am the Lord, and there is none else, there is no
God beside me: I girded thee, though thou hast not
known me:
That they may know from the rising of the sun, and
from the west, that there is none beside me. I am
the Lord . . .

ISAIAH 45:5,6

Blessed be the name of the Lord from this time
forth and for evermore.
From the rising of the sun unto the going down of
the same the Lord's name is to be praised.

PSALM 113: 2,3

And he shall be as the light of the morning,
when the sun riseth, even a morning without clouds;
as the tender grass springing out of the earth
by clear shining after rain.

II SAMUEL 23:4

Praised be my Lord for our sister the
moon, and for the stars, the which
he has set clear and lovely in heaven.

He appointed the moon for seasons: the sun
knoweth his going down.
Thou makest darkness, and it is night: wherein all
the beasts of the forest do creep forth.
The young lions roar after their prey, and seek
their meat from God.
The sun ariseth, they gather themselves together,
and lay them down in their dens.
O Lord, how manifold are thy works!
in wisdom hast thou made them all: the earth
is full of thy riches.

PSALM 104:19-22,24

When I consider thy heavens, the work of thy
fingers, the moon and the stars, which thou hast
ordained;
What is man, that thou art mindful of him? and the
son of man, that thou visitest him?

PSALM 8:3,4

. . . Blessed of the Lord be his land, for the precious
things of heaven, for the dew, and for the deep
that coucheth beneath,
And for the precious fruits brought forth by the sun,
and for the precious things put forth by the moon . .

DEUTERONOMY 33:13,14

Praise ye the Lord: for it is good to sing praises
unto our God . . .
He telleth the number of the stars; he calleth them
all by their names.
Great is our Lord, and of great power: his
understanding is infinite.

PSALM 147:1,4,5

*Praised be my Lord for our brother
the wind, and for air and cloud,
calms and all weather, by the which
thou upholdest in life all creatures.*

Bless the Lord, O my soul. O Lord my God, thou art
very great; thou art clothed with honour and majesty.
Who coverest thyself with light as with a garment:
who stretchest out the heavens like a curtain:
Who layeth the beams of his chambers in the waters:
who maketh the clouds his chariot: who walketh upon
the wings of the wind.

PSALM 104: 1-3

Ask ye of the Lord rain in the time of the latter
rain; so the Lord shall make bright clouds, and
give them showers of rain, to every one
grass in the field.

ZECHARIAH 10:1

Sing unto the Lord with thanksgiving . . .
Who covereth the heaven with clouds, who prepareth
rain for the earth, who maketh grass to grow upon the
mountains.

PSALM 147:7,8

I will extol thee, my God, O king; and I will bless
thy name for ever and ever.
Every day will I bless thee; and I will praise thy
name for ever and ever.
Great is the Lord, and greatly to be praised;
and his greatness is unsearchable.
I will speak of the glorious honour of thy majesty,
and of thy wondrous works.

PSALM 145: 1-3, 5

Praised be my Lord for our sister water,
who is very serviceable unto us, and
humble, and precious, and clean.

Who laid the foundations of the earth, that it should
not be removed for ever.
Thou coveredst it with the deep as with a garment: the
waters stood above the mountains.
He sendeth the springs into the valleys, which run
among the hills.
They give drink to every beast of the field: the
wild asses quench their thirst.
By them shall the fowls of the heaven have their
habitation, which sing among the branches.

PSALM 104:5,6,10-12

When the poor and needy seek water, and there is
none, and their tongue faileth for thirst, I the
Lord will hear them, I the God of Israel will not
forsake them.
I will open rivers in high places, and fountains
in the midst of the valleys: I will make the wilderness a pool of water, and the dry land
springs of water.

ISAIAH 41:17,18

He turneth the wilderness into a standing water,
and dry ground into watersprings.
And there he maketh the hungry to dwell . . .

PSALM 107:35,36

. . . the desert shall rejoice, and blossom as the rose.
And the parched ground shall become a pool,
and the thirsty land springs of water . . .

ISAIAH 35:1,7

Praised be my Lord for our brother
fire, through whom thou givest us
light in the darkness; and he is bright,
and pleasant, and very mighty.
            and strong.

If thy whole body therefore be full of light, having
no part dark, the whole shall be full of light, as
when the bright shining of a candle
doth give thee light.

LUKE 11: 36

For thou wilt light my candle: the Lord my God will
enlighten my darkness.

PSALM 18:28

. . . I will not rest, until the righteousness thereof
go forth as brightness, and the salvation thereof as
a lamp that burneth.

ISAIAH 62:1

And there were many lights in the upper chamber,
where they were gathered together.

ACTS 20:8

No man, when he hath lighted a candle, covereth it
with a vessel, or putteth it under a bed; but
setteth it on a candlestick, that they which enter in
may see the light.

LUKE 8: 16

And he put the candlestick
in the tent of the congregation . . .
And he lighted the lamps before the Lord . . .

EXODUS 40:24,25

Praised be my Lord for our mother the earth, the which doth sustain us and keep us...

The heaven, even the heavens, are the Lord's:
but the earth hath he given to the children of men.

PSALM 115:16

. . . he will love thee, and bless thee, and multiply
thee: he will also bless the fruit of thy womb, and
the fruit of thy land, thy corn, and thy wine, and
thine oil, the increase of thy kine, and the flocks
of thy sheep . . .

DEUTERONOMY 7:13

While the earth remaineth, seedtime and harvest,
and cold and heat, and summer and winter, and
day and night shall not cease.

GENESIS 8:22

Thou visitest the earth, and waterest it: thou
greatly enrichest it with the river of God, which is
full of water: thou preparest them corn, when thou
hast so provided for it.
Thou waterest the ridges thereof abundantly: thou
settlest the furrows thereof: thou makest it soft with
showers: thou blessest the springing thereof.
Thou crownest the year with thy goodness . . .
The pastures are clothed with flocks; the valleys also
are covered over with corn; they shout for joy, they
also sing.

PSALM 65:9-11,13

...and bringeth forth divers fruits,
and flowers of many colors,
and grass.

And God said, Let the earth bring forth grass, the
herb yielding seed, and the fruit tree yielding
fruit after his kind, whose seed is in itself, upon
the earth: and it was so.

GENESIS 1:11

For the Lord thy God bringeth thee into a good land,
a land of brooks of water, of fountains and depths
that spring out of valleys and hills;
A land of wheat, and barley, and vines, and fig
trees, and pomegranates; a land of oil olive, and
honey.

DEUTERONOMY 8:7,8

He watereth the hills from his chambers: the earth
is satisfied with the fruit of thy works.
He causeth the grass to grow for the cattle, and
herb for the service of man: that he may bring
forth food out of the earth;
And wine that maketh glad the heart of man,
and oil to make his face to shine, and bread which
strengtheneth man's heart.
The trees of the Lord are full of sap; the cedars
of Lebanon, which he hath planted;
Where the birds make their nests: as for the stork,
the fir trees are her house.
The high hills are a refuge for the wild goats; and
the rocks for the conies.

PSALM 104:13-18

. . . Consider the lilies of the field, how they grow;
they toil not, neither do they spin:
And yet I say unto you, That even Solomon in all his
glory was not arrayed like one of these.

MATTHEW 6:28,29

Praised be my Lord for all those
who pardon one another for his
love's sake and who endure
weakness and tribulation;...

Blessed be God, even the Father of our Lord Jesus
Christ, the Father of mercies, and the God of all
comfort;
Who comforteth us in all our tribulation,
that we may be able to comfort them which are in
any trouble, by the comfort wherewith we ourselves
are comforted of God.

II CORINTHIANS 1:3,4

Be kindly affectioned one to another with brotherly
love; in honour preferring one another;
Rejoicing in hope; patient in tribution; continuing
instant in prayer . . .

ROMANS 12:10,12

. . . if we walk in the light, as he is in the light,
we have fellowship one with another, and the blood
of Jesus Christ his Son cleanseth us from all sin.

I JOHN 1:7

And he said unto me, My grace is sufficient for
thee: for my strength is made perfect in weakness.
Most gladly therefore will I rather glory in my in-
firmities, that the power of Christ may rest upon me.

II CORINTHIANS 12:9

Sing, O heavens; and be joyful, O earth; and break
forth into singing, O mountains: for the Lord hath
comforted his people, and will have mercy upon his
afflicted.

ISAIAH 49:13

...blessed are they who peaceably
shall endure, for thou,
O most Highest,
        shalt give them a crown!

These things I have spoken unto you, that in me ye might have peace. In the world ye shall have tribulation: but be of good cheer; I have overcome the world.

JOHN 16:33

For his anger endureth but a moment; in his favour is life: weeping may endure for a night, but joy cometh in the morning.

PSALM 30:5

Blessed is the man that endureth temptation: for when he is tried, he shall receive the crown of life, which the Lord hath promised to them that love him.

JAMES 1:12

Henceforth there is laid up for me a crown of righteousness, which the Lord, the righteous judge, shall give me at that day: and not to me only, but unto all them also that love his appearing.

II TIMOTHY 4:8

And when the chief Shepherd shall appear, ye shall receive a crown of glory that fadeth not away.

I PETER 5:4

Cast thy burden upon the Lord, and he shall sustain thee: he shall never suffer the righteous to be moved.

PSALM 55:22

Praised be my Lord for our sister,
the death of the body, from whom
no man escapeth.

Jesus said unto her, I am the resurrection, and the
life: he that believeth in me, though he were dead,
yet shall he live:
And whosoever liveth and believeth
in me shall never die . . .

JOHN 11:25,26

Herein is love, not that we loved God, but that he
loved us, and sent his Son to be the propitiation
for our sins.
Beloved, if God so loved us, we ought also to
love one another.

I JOHN 4:10,11

The next day John seeth Jesus coming unto him, and
saith, Behold the Lamb of God, which taketh away
the sin of the world.

JOHN 1:29

For God so loved the world, that he gave his only
begotten Son, that whosoever believeth in him
should not perish, but have everlasting life.

JOHN 3:16

Blessed be the God and Father of our Lord Jesus
Christ, which according to his abundant mercy hath
begotten us again unto a lively hope by the resurrection of Jesus Christ from the dead.

I PETER 1:3

Praise ye, and bless ye the Lord,
and give thanks unto him, and
serve him with great humility.

St. Francis of Assisi

The Lord is gracious, and full of compassion; slow
to anger, and of great mercy.
The Lord is good to all: and his tender mercies are
over all his works.
Thy kingdom is an everlasting kingdom, and thy
dominion endureth throughout all generations.
The Lord upholdeth all that fall, and raiseth up
all those that be bowed down.
The Lord is righteous in all his ways, and holy
in all his works.
The Lord is nigh unto all them that call upon him,
to all that call upon him in truth.

PSALM 145:8,9,13,14,17.18

Make a joyful noise unto the Lord, all ye lands.
Serve the Lord with gladness: come before his
presence with singing.
Know ye that the Lord he is God: it is he that
hath made us, and not we ourselves; we are his
people, and the sheep of his pasture.
Enter into his gates with thanksgiving, and into
his courts with praise: be thankful unto him, and
bless his name.
For the Lord is good; his mercy is everlasting; and
his truth endureth to all generations.

PSALM 100

O praise the Lord, all ye nations: praise him,
all ye people.
For his merciful kindness is great toward us: and
the truth of the Lord endureth for ever. Praise ye
the Lord.

PSALM 117